Dancing
With
Skeletons

A collection of works by the H.U.N.

«While all bodies share the same fate
all voices do not.»

- Li Young-Lee

Dancing With Skeletons

A collection of works by the H.U.N.

Dancing with Skeletons
A collection of works by the H.U.N.
First Printing: 2011

ISBN - 13: 978-1463661748
ISBN - 10: 1463661746

Pseudo Poseur Productions
116 W. 12th St.
Wayne, Ne 68787
America

www.pseudoposeur.com

Cover art by Liz Lofgren
Back cover art by Brian Finn
Editor: Alex West
Cover & book design: Pseudo Poseur Productions

TABLE OF CONTENTS

Alvaro Archundia Perez   61

David Dietz 119

Foreward

It's very telling that writing this foreword is the first real writing I've done since my family's move to Oregon. That's because, at the heart of the writing group that is the House of United Nations, is a philosophy that states, in part, "Thou shalt write." And that's the point: the House of United Nations has many "rules" but the chief amongst them is to write. Write to the best of your ability, and respect the written word. And by not writing, am I—or the audience of this book—following the rules of being a writer?

I remember the HUN in its infancy. It was really the idea of Zach Drees, although he'll always contest that I had some influence on the group's creation. And when it began, I remember hoping—praying, honestly—that it would become what it needed to become: a haven for poets of all genres, races, ethnicities, sexual orientations—everything a broken America promised it would be to its citizens, everything the fake United Nations promised, in a way, to the world. The House of United Nations needed to be willing to not only vigorously write and write well, but also to perform outreach, mentorship of not only poets, but people, promotion of poetry in general and good poetry in particular—all the while being not merely a place, but an idea that could easily be transported to anywhere in the world. And while the world hasn't had a chance to sit down with the unique, powerful and humble voices that make up the HUN, this volume of poems from the Initiating Class (OHUNIC, nigga) puts the world on notice:

The House of United Nations is here. They are bold. They risk everything—and I mean everything—with every poem. They are organized, and willing to promote their craft and the cause of poetry at the drop of a hat (even a fedora). They work with youth, regardless of perceived social standing, race or religion. They despise inequality at every turn. They inspire. They produce. They eat. They let people I love realize there is value in themselves. They don't judge. They keep it very, very real. If love were a terrorist ideal, they would be stone cold terrorists.

And I love every one of them.

Above, I said that the chief rule of the HUN is to write, write well and respect writing. I think I was wrong, and I'm glad I was. I think, at the heart of the HUN, is a grander rule. One that is more important—in fact, one that everyone on the planet should abide by. And that rule is, simply, "Be Cool." This is why I love the HUN. This is why they are my family.

So here are some poems. Really good ones, too. For once, you didn't waste your money. That has to feel good. Congrats!

And hey, if you like what you read, (or need it explained, or want to hear it live) why don't you join? You don't have to be a writer. But be warned: the House of United Nations will make a writer out of you. They will also make a friend out of you. And man, that's what being cool is all about.

Enjoy.

--Timothy Black
Author of *Connecticut Shade*
Cave Canem Poet
Honorary HUN Poet

Dancing With Skeletons

A collection of works by the H.U.N.

Zach
Drees

"It is the mark of an educated mind to be able to entertain a thought without accepting it."

- Aristotle

Too Familiar to be Forgotten
by Zach Drees

Sirens sing dirges as
red and blue pierce black.

T-shirt torn, sweaty and stained,
he wonders who else drew the short straw tonight.

Mind racing, ringing only
that constant fear,
that fear,
that *fear!*

An eight by ten cell, solitude, sodomy--
no tweaking to numbness...

If he could just *focus*
he could *remember.*

Closed eyes recall crystals,
burning tongue and God.
A knock at the door,
so loud
so loud
so *loud!*

Terrified, tense,
a broken bottle,
secure,
knob turns

nothing.

Awaken, and trembles begin,
bottle slips to quicksand cement.

The blood on his shirt
belongs to another,
last words of his victim,
I love you,
brother.

Progress?
by Zach Drees

Another skyscraper, cement and steel,
it only cost a few lives.

Structurally sound, unstable stability,
shatters like Chinaware at the
whisper of an inquisitive mind.

Seeing untouched, uncorrupted, nothing
he lights a cigarette over spreading flame,
dances to distant sirens,
and laughs at how fast the treated wood burns.

Eye of Providence
by Zach Drees

Your golden band will
bruise her breasts;
your violent penetration,
a dagger, drawing blood.

All take a turn,
President through Priest.
From behind, because
innocent eyes imprison.

Exhausted, she falls limp;
you ejaculate her last rites.

A latex defense,
Benjamin bandages,
a meal for her child.

Father told you,
pray and be forgiven.

Your unborn fetus,
defiles The Virgin
in your mother's garden.

The Beginning
by Zach Drees

Nephele shrouds the night's eyes--
the reflection of dashboard lights,
a poor substitute.

He came in the rain, seeking shelter,
to speak his news in the home of his brother.

His shirt was stained with blood and earth,
a portrait of inevitable immortal corruption.
They came from the trees,
he said,
from the branches and beyond.
Eyes hollow,
teeth rotting from
ammonia and ether,
they wielded weapons--
a deluded desire for glory.
One of his own had fallen prey to these beasts--
blood, fertilizer,
birthing fury by terror in the soul of a child.
Eerily calm,
his voice never wavers,
veiling purpose in vain--
his eyes plead the favor
his pride disallows.

Relieved of his tale,
the adolescent rests,
finding solace in the silence
of his brother,
his keeper.

A crossroads created
by fallible fate--

strive forward in selfishness,
or return to ball and chain,
a slave, a savior from
acquiescence.

Another whiskey,
an attempt at a wretched sleep,
fails,
for the immortal within
allows no peace.

The thunder fades,
and the storm begins.

The Speaker
by Zach Drees

He walked in smelling of herb
and menthol cigarette smoke.

A leather jacket and blue-jeans--
odd attire for such a formal function.

He carried no notes--
his stride to the mic
bearing confidence
in their lack of necessity.
Scattered applause,
silenced by a humble
smile into the podium.
A smile found only in blind children
and the senility of the old.

Fixated by his eyes,
seemingly void
of a decided hue.
Perhaps red, burning red--
roses blossom in a thicket of thorns.
The movement of his lips,
coaxing the echoing words,
as he spoke with profound passion
of an evolved resilience to conformity,
to subservience,
in a possessed society.
The lighting of a cigarette,
general disregard for the signs
well within his view.
He neither pleaded nor begged,
relying on the eminence
of epiphany alone.
Mothers reach in vain

to shelter their kin,
suddenly lured to father's pitchfork.

When finished,
he drops his cigarette,
and walks out of the building,
leaving shattered thorns in a
sea of awakened rose buds.

Punitive Naiveté

by Zach Drees

A midnight phone call bears sorrow
to the widowed Mother of Men.
Her tears fall to the asphalt,
stained with the blood of a child astray,
his pistol imparts the façade of a man.
A pawn, lost in a masquerade,
romanticized by the lure of heroic menace.
Naiveté is not freed by apology
for one of the Young Brethren,
liberated only by death
in this war devoid of victory.

A Call From Home

by Zach Drees

She cries the tears he refuses to shed,
minutes of silence, a lifetime.

She can still hear the words
he tried so hard to muffle,
seeping from the light of his cell phone.

They took him from us, man
killed 'im 'cause they could.
Drink one for the fallen.

Gaze void of emotion, transfixed upon nothing,
he writes without words,
while the cursed messenger blinks dirges
into the coffee table.

His calm state frightens her,
compassion so hollowed
he must be Death or God.

Reading her fear, he whispers,
echoing explanation,
caressing grief,

It coulda been family babe,
it coulda been family.

Virtuoso

by Zach Drees

Rejected by sleep, retreat to a cellar
hidden under the floorboards
of the rotting tool shed.

Cloaked, guise of an artist,
find a soul, *our soul,*
dangles from rusted hooks,
alive but asleep,
scarred beyond recognition.

A lone, flickering bulb
reveals a fresh canvas
below the feeble entity,
rag and razor begin today's portrait.

What is seen, thin slice of eyelid,
heard, tip of an ear,
and for what is felt, withheld instinct,
a gash along the shaft of the semi-erect penis.

Release by indifference, insanity--
spread the blood of this disturbed masterpiece.

Self-Inflicted

by Zach Drees

Sinners scream *sinner!*
while saints screw the wives

None remain to plead forgiveness.

All that was is lost
submerged in a sea
of silent sorrow,

our God reincarnated
as a cockroach.

The Poet
by Zach Drees

Eyesight taken by debt,
he shields sockets behind shades,
smoke from his cigarette
adding to the haze of the dimly-lit bar.

Reaching for the mic,
he cradles it softly,
an infant with a bottle.

Lips so close,
the crowded room breathes for him,
living and dying with each whispered word.

From knowing all to knowing nothing,
and wiser,
in that final, trailing line.

Skin chilled, awaken immortal,
while Lucifer himself cowers in the corner.

Waiting For Paradise

by Zach Drees

It was all a show,
without an audience.
Her insistent silence,
inciting a tirade,
birthing a beating.

A whisper
from swollen lips,
deafening with
words never spoken.

My story?
You want to know
my story?

Born to a whore in a
subway bathroom stall.
If only mother's mercy
had drowned me
in the toilet that night.

No father--
fill-ins to rape and beat me.
At four, one of them
pierced my purity,
tossing my nude
carcass into
mother's needle.

Such satisfying pain.

A callow child,
I ached for Mother's
lips on my wound,

illusive asylum.

I found her in front
of the bathroom mirror,
voiceless,
waiting for paradise.

At sixteen, I escaped
to purgatorial torment.
Poorer than my
addict mother, to
emerge not of her
but as her.

And you.
Who the fuck are you?

Three crystal lines up,
he has heard not a word,
only *The Pusher,*
enchanting from
the headphones in the
Ipod across the room.

Left alone in her grief,
a powder laden razor
sacrifices another lamb.

Immortal abandonment,
her blood-stained figure,
lifeless, a playground for
the crystallized beast.

A line off each of her
pale, maternal breasts,
he parts her legs and
slides in,

such satisfying pain.

The taste of salt
and red wine
only feeds the
repressed madness.

His blood?
Her blood?

Were they not one?

One more line,
a final thrust,
razor in hand,
waiting for paradise.

Blitzkrieg
by Zach Drees

Releasing eyes from the monitor,
he scans each plaque, each degree,
still just paper on a wall.

Words echo through years,
from that day of caps and gowns,
pierce his subconscious,
refusing imprisonment in a high school gymnasium.
That boy, the thin one there,
loose cannon, always stirring things up.
Damn shame too,
could go to Harvard,
he'll end up in prison.

Nods of agreement from none who knew,
tasting sour superiority.

Now resilience powers his ink-laden barrel,
pointed at the foot of their precious pedestal.

Demonic Chastity

by Zach Drees

Acquitted by negligence,
he carefully begins his masterpiece.
The silky fur of the mane, gentle paws,
celestial whiskers.
A high-pitched giggle,
silenced by a divine infatuation
with those entrancing blue eyes.

A child's demonic chastity.
For the soul, a cell,
or a sanctuary?

A twitch of a tail,
the dental-floss noose
denying the last purrs of protest.
The blue eyes are bursting now,
red with salty Merlot.
It pools with the seeping feces--
Sodomized by the protruding crucifix,

The unpinned Savior, pleading,
arm outstretched,
groping blindly for absolution.

Innocence Lost

by Zach Drees

Winter's stare of judgment descends upon us,
as the last leaf of innocence falls neglected to the frozen earth.
Innocence lost is a young girl on prom night,
blissfully comatose through her drunken deflowering.
Desperation drowns her in the tears of her unborn child,
her fears of conviction liberated by a syringe.

A child birthed in a dumpster,
his skull crushed on a stone.

Relieved of her shackles of sin,
she thirsts for the pinch of the nylon,
and the prick of the needle.
She cannot shed a tear,
as the sunset fades over the horizon.
Bear witness to the falling of a lamb.

The Rebirth

by Zach Drees

There is no woman to console him,
in his destitute, one-bedroom flat;
love is reserved for the affluent.
He soothes his hands with rust,
numbing the assembly-line calluses,
messianic mountains.
A newspaper shields his fragile figure,
a bottle his only ally.
Mercy abides in
a euphoric dream,
the anguish of a fleeting utopia
reviving the immortal soul.

He bows his head to the flame,
amusing his nicotine lust.
The sunken eyes lift,
and the cigarette slides from his lips,
igniting the streets with Black Flame.
His laughter echoes,
as the shirtless and shoeless
empty into the streets.
In front of him, a crumbling hypocrisy;
Behind him, an army, awake with defiance.

Tune-in

by Zach Drees

Fox News
That forced, overly iconic voice,
cult-like, almost religious,
and he can't help but roll his eyes.

Ok, tell us why those blue and red arrows
on that grid in your background,
never fail to be falling.

Ahh, but first you will preach
venomous words of promise,
narrowing to a barricade
built in the haste of a coward.

Drag us to your playing field,
a booby-trapped safe-haven,
and begin your slaughter but know,
where others are water I am stone.

Go ahead, attempt to explain
how a tax break on the rich
will save our plummeting economy--
I wonder if the girl licking crumbs
in the dumpster behind your
overpriced, "gourmet" restaurant would agree.

Drop to your knees, you pathetic, suit-wearing fuck,
suck the dick of capitalism, smile while you do it,
swallow, tell me you enjoy it.

You are the worst of men, a parasite
feeding on his own, spitting lies
for a paycheck.

Go ahead, flap those lips to your
collected, implanted imagination,
but check your Rolex, friend,
for I too am at home in the lion's den.

Alley Preacher

by Zach Drees

The problem with this country
he says
sipping sin from a bottle while
sucking down a menthol cigarette
has nothing to do with the leaders
the figureheads
the puppets of the monopolized corporation,
nor the system holding secrets from the fucking people.

One trait holds prevalent over the rest.
One trait glorified by our species alone.

He pauses for anticipation
for the sweat
for a sweet shot of knowledge in a swig from the bottle.

Laziness
he says
pausing again for effect
lights a cigarette from the butt of the last
and repeats
Laziness
indifference
a goddamn sheep-in-a-pen attitude.

That's the problem today, man
everyone only pretends to protest
to revolt
to fucking evolve, man
to take that risk
dig through shit
and hope to find gold
but nobody
not a soul

has the balls
the kahones
the fucking self-pride

to flip the cards
go all in
ride it all on a hope for something more.

Conscience

by Zach Drees

He never understood how steel in flesh brought warmth,
not comforting, more piercing,
like the last whiskey of a long night.
Or how the butt of a menthol cigarette
could burn so perfectly through unconscious flesh,
opening to ooze like candle wax.

Eyes ablaze, he bolts upright in bed,
drenched and panting,
struggling to restrain his thrashing heart.

How do I know that? Only he *could know that,*
the unlucky one, who should've walked away.

Memory, the state of psychosis,
remedied with denial,
further psychotic disillusionment.

He's awakened her, the blue-eyed angel
beside him, her feather fingertips
dance from cheek to chest and back,
lighthearted as children on the first day of summer.

She wants him to sleep,
to dream of glory, peace, and love.

She wants him to wake smiling each morning,
and to look in the mirror without disgust.

He wonders if she feels the scars in him,
so raw its war to conceal them.

He wonders if she is freed in her innocent dreams,
the way he is imprisoned by his,

he wonders if she wonders
why his pace still quickens at the sound of sirens.

Pondering Mushin

by Zach Drees

"Life is a tragedy for those who feel, but a comedy to those who think."
--Horace Walpole

The midnight hour welcomes footsteps,
too engrossed in thought to worship time.
Seek sovereignty in the mind,
where two paths are traveled as one,
no crevice too wide to bridge.

Is man's insight on evil
no more than fallible belief?

> *Is the dandelion insulted by the*
> *shy caress of the wasp?*

Did He give us free-will
to will against him?

> *Do the wings of the hummingbird*
> *disturb the ears of the field mouse?*

A leaf from the ancient white oak drifts,
wandering but never grounding,
the forgotten philosopher poet.

The Speaker Has the Floor
by Zach Drees

Puppets preach legislation
to a council of chess pieces--
the microphone, a plastic inflatable.

Words within walls are carefully measured,
churned softly to poison,
spoon-fed to a society too naked to notice.

Bomb here, drill there--
bury them in closed caskets,
it's easier that way.

Make it home every night for dinner with the wife,
but wonder why the son does not speak.

The son who reads Marx, Malcolm, and Plato.

The son who learned how to shoot up a school
from late night HBO.

The son who understands
why the snowflake clings so desperate to the pine needle.

To a Generation
by Zach Drees

He plays the butterfly blade
smooth as any sax solo,
each flip, turn, a rhythm
to the twisted tune of his world.

Secret was to let you hand loose,
allow the blade to roll over your knuckles,
trust in your superiority over a tool.

He believes the mind must work as such.

But free thinking is forbidden,
just watch your evening news,
not by institutional law,
rather by social estrangement.

Fucking communist.

Join the few, roar revolution--
know on each returning howl
rides a dozen whispers of your fall.

Work your mind as you work the blade--
know it may only be an exercise.

Do not restrict your gaze
to the path carved by your predecessors,
for those who have failed before
are bare, brittle trees falling
as we sprout from their remains.

Liz Lofgren

"no tears in the writer, no tears in the reader."

- Robert Frost

Dusty Roads

by Liz Lofgren

Maybe one day as the mind expands,
I'll get up and take your hand.
The only thing I'm sure about
is how I'll never understand.

As fate wills me to get out,
only you can hear me shout;
come outside and see what lies,
see what *peace* can bring about.

I know it when I see your eyes
the happy end when freedom cries.
Come stand with me and hear its call,
the will, the spirit never dies.

Yet as I walk this narrow wall,
balance fails, and I will fall.
I'm just a pothead, nothing more.
I haven't changed the world at all.

What I ask is not a chore,
but to be part of something more.
REVOLUTION stirs awake,
and in that thought I shall adore.

The minds that recognize the fake
have choices spread throughout their wake.
So stand up as I take your hand,
and simply smile as dawn awaits.

Devotion
by Liz Lofgren

wash the dirt away
still some lingers, never gone
endlessly scrubbing

Expressions
by Liz Lofgren

How do we understand the paradox of individualism held
    within secularism?
To claim to be distinctive, exclusive, and unique,
yet all painted as one big white-washed patriotic whole?
How to be distinctive and yet all be one in the same,
a mass of unique colors that eventually bleed together into a
    lifeless brown?
How to win a fight for attention when all others wear the same
    creative mask as you?
What's *your* attention-getter in this extemporaneous speech of
    life?

Well, sex truly is the life-drive and focus of existence
    nowadays,
so I won't *beat around the bush.*
By using strong undertones, I could express sexual repression
and manifest excitement in your unremitting Freudian battle.
I could morph a classy sexual reference into tasteless shouts of
    profanity,
taboos of rape, and fucking, and choking chickens, and sluts
    with cunts
and dildos in a dresser drawer!
Look at me, I'm hollering about cocks, bitches, shit, fuck fuck
look at me
look at me
LOOK AT ME!

Or,
realizing the tackiness of it all,
I could fly off on a tangent rampage.
I could point fingers at fat and balding covetous pigs in city
    hall,
having their huge offices and houses and fancy cars
that serve to compensate for their lack of . . . something else.

I could rage about fraud and money-laundering,
the use of doublespeak to justify wars of genocide and
        persecution,
point out the gaping holes in organized religion that it
        brain-washes its zombies not to see.
I could unleash a wrath of blind fury on my resentment
for ethnocentric military power with the apparent divine right
to establish uninterrupted religious and political authority
in a nation we label as 'free'.

Fuck it.
How about I just chill the fuck out,
take it down a couple notches, try out these things they call
their j's,
their pinners, their doobies, their sticks, their cheeches, their
        fatties, their damn hippie cigarettes.
Mellow out after another shitty day at your shitty job.
Get lifted, blitzed, stoned, high, blazed, torched, buzzed,
        plowed, loaded, toasted, lit, ripped.
Find your bonsai tree and search for that state of nothingness,
zero stimuli,
your own makeshift nirvana in a world of idolized objects.
Surf chills that overwhelm your body with ecstasy.
Close your eyes and feel your soul roll backwards into a
        cosmic realm
where time nor space exists,
only you.
Open your mind and have endless epiphanies of the very
        essence of life,
only to forget them once you've come down.

What if your poison of choice isn't pot, but something else?
Maybe try some harder things, just to have that experience of a
        good time.
What happens when the reason changes
from having an experience to having an escape?
What happens when you no longer have control of when you

want your fix?
What will you do when you wake up in the middle of the night
your body trembling uncontrollably,
involuntary shakes so intense that they throw you from the bed,
spasms so violent it leaves you powerless to even utter a single
        whimper of distress?
What are you going to do when your ice dealer is out of town?

We've all had those sleepless nights when you contemplated
the pros and cons of never waking up again. What's the point?
I could try to convey a feeling of pain so deep and sincere
that it goes beyond guttural sobs and frustrated shrieks of
        agony,
pain that can drive you to claw at your own body,
to see just how far you can dig your nails in to peel up the skin,
a fruitless attempt to dissipate the grief within your tired soul
        into something more corporeal.
Lacerate your entire body, all to allow your step into a new
bruised and bleeding coat of hellish content
in hopes that you can slip for one moment—
one solitary moment
away from the unfathomable logics of gravity and time.
Whatever nameless anguish you may suffer could aim to
        dissolve
within the bleeding folded recess of your slowly dying self.

Any of this sound familiar?
Of course it does.
Sex, anger, euphoria, contentment, despair, love and hate,
        abandonment,
they're all universal.
We are connected by these primitive traits that set us apart from
        beasts.
Society traps people in impenetrable, suffocating boxes using
        categories and labels,
and it suppresses any true individualism and freedom they
        might have once had.

39

Put the focus on what brings us together, what we have in
      common, not what makes us different.
I'm tired of using seemingly superfluous streams of poetry to
      enhance the message here.
We are all linked, we are all connected.

No one is alone.

Insomnia

by Liz Lofgren

Shadows sulk this haunting midnight hour.
I lay robbed of dreams,
the bed an empty expanse,
a desolate ocean, unending
extending to the edge of existence.
I float lost,
my life jacket—his sweater,
his scent, faint
woven within the fibers themselves.
That scent grabs my sanity
before I fall to the abyss
beyond the edge of the world.
I curl inside this sweater cocoon,
stroke the sheet where he should have slept
and wait for the sunrise
of tomorrow's horizon
when he, my island, my continent,
can fill the void in this ocean,
this bed,
all shadows diffuse in the wake of my dreams.

Piano Concerto No. 69

by Liz Lofgren

Inside an empty concert hall,
a piano sat in quiet patience,
forgotten amidst dusty air
on a barren center stage.
The lights turned up,
and the pianist took proud strides
toward his quiet subject.

He did not sit down at first.
He walked around her, studied her,
traced his slender fingers across her back,
falling in lust with her sleek blackness.
The pianist finished eyeing her,
and pulled out the bench
with a gentle scrape across the floor.
He lifted up the cover,
and she greeted him with an ivory smile.
He fingered the keys,
anticipation building with every touch.

He started slow; a soft, drifting melody
hummed from vibrating chords.
Her song was beautiful and sweet,
seducing him to play more.
He teased her with tensions and resolutions,
crescendos and diminuendos.
Thrusting forward and backward on the bench,
his strong fingers played harder and faster,
harder and faster.
He stretched through her whole range of notes
and pounded through his song.
Intensity building, he broke a sweat
as she sang louder and louder.
His fingers danced over her,

their rhythms in sync.
The music surged harder and harder, and then—
a final blow to the keys
came as the song's climax.
She screamed her finishing chords.

He held those notes down
until the last ringing echo
faded into nothingness.
Breathing hard, he sat for a moment
before finally removing his hands.
He placed the cover on her tired keys,
and lit up a smoke as he leaned back on the bench.

Adam's Ale
by Liz Lofgren

Birth.
Snowflakes ride on soft winds
and kiss the mountain peak,
wind gently caresses innocence
on infant's cheek.
Untouched by demons, world pure
quiet like souls of ancient trees,
roots woven deep into mountain rock.
Too quickly turns to blistering reality--
the world is revealed.

Infants, snowflakes scooped,
carried down the mountain by winds of wisdom
and child succumbs to adolescence
as snowflakes melt in acquiescence.
A child's mind absolute and free,
like the river's unending kinetic energy.
Collective unconscious fuels
the strength of the river, forever bound
in quest to seek low ground.

Elevation lowers, as imagination diminishes
River turned to creek,
to trickle,
to nothing.
None see it coming.
Losing strength, no longer a child,
he never knew to run.

Oceans of conformity enlist with open arms
all pollution-saturated driplets of water,
every lost and tired man
longing for acceptance.
Pooled together, all are bred the same
drift the same

wave the same
lame ducks in a sea of unoriginality.

Will you let this be your fate?
Downfall will not be unwilling,
but hopeless
passion dead by the roadside
forgotten.
Do not be drug down by the fallen.
Shed all filth that pollutes the mind,
tear apart all that binds,
break down everything you think you know
and you will find

Enlightenment.

Evaporate from seas of negativity
elevate to the heavens
shake hands with destiny
manifest.
Condense into storm clouds,
unleash torrents of fury
wash away toxicity,
flounder wastelands in heresy,
pursue knowledge, clarity.
Perception *is* reality.

We can birth to snowflake innocence,
melt in rivers of absolution
and generations to come
will bask in bliss existence.

Shangri-la

by Liz Lofgren

Alone I sit
on ancient banks in a world lost
Silent, secure
Lake glitters salmon sunset

Thunder rolls, shatters silence
earth's hearbeat, bassline of life
Citrus rains sprinkle dainty drops
on the lake surface

Winds from high mountains
bristle gently through trees—
maracas in the distance
as pine scents dance through the air

I stare, mesmerized
by snare taps of rain
Ripples caused not by angel's tears
but thousands of fish racing up
to kiss the surface

And as trees dance and fish make love
waves gyrate the mountain's reflection
nature's equalizer

Far from silence, I close my eyes
inhale music of the earth
I am free

Resolution
by Liz Lofgren

Morning sun,
rub sleep from his eyes.
Peek over pink horizon,
illuminate dew drops
in languid summer grass—
a million tiny prisms aglow.
Sweet caress of morning breeze
carries scents of last night's
love's first summer sunset kiss.

Life radiates magnificence
from heaven's palette to insect's wing,
yet dwarfed by the cosmos
that radiates from his eyes.
I travel galaxies in a single shared glance.

I wait in dreams of salmon sunrise
for reunion of lonely lips.
The tranquil morning is timeless,
as I gaze lost in dawn's first light.

Diamond Skies
by Liz Lofgren

He pressed me close—
lost in eyes of cobalt sea.
His flame reignites passion.
Together, we confirm destiny.

Furious monsoon of ideas
wash away all corruption,
lifejacket words thrown
to those desperately drowning.
Beam atop Pharos
guides the blind out of the fog.

From murky nightmares
of existence's spiral of destruction,
his words pull me back
and I am at peace.
Why not us?

This is the calm before the storm.

To-Die-Fors

by Liz Lofgren

Consumer zombies devotedly carry out
daily pious rituals in churches
malls and dollar stores,
paradox of idolatry
in a godless religion.

Thrown to their knees, bow to desire,
the need of these things,
these things, these *things*,
the must-haves, the so-cutes,
the can't-live-withouts.

Bigoted, self-righteous way of thinking,
way of *life*
can be ripped apart as easily
as tearing through the green bits of paper
so dearly worshipped

Good Morals mass produced,
imported from China,
unique and creative
exactly like the neighbors'.

On a thrift-store shelf
sits a forgotten emblem of love—
a dusty clay pot
thrown by someone's great-great-
great-great-granddad.

Yet a careless elbow knocks—murders,
the last of family traditions
shatters on sterile linoleum
just as dandelions choke on pesticides,
crying out in a sea of manicured lawns.

Last chance at color in a grayscale world
withers from existence.

Fading

by Liz Lofgren

Sweat, fresh from morning's jog,
burns frantic eyes as she searches
the crowded emergency room.
Worries vanish as she's greeted
by beaming father in hospital scrubs,
cradling his sleeping infant.

Both child and grandmother are born.

Her wrinkled hands reach
for the bundle of innocence.
Marveling blue eyes open at Grandma's touch.
Tearful smile wonders
Who's this beautiful little princess?

Wincing at age's toll,
she struggles out of the Crown Vic.
Blonde ringlets bounce in step
to greet Grandma with shrieking laughter.
Armed with cake topped with six unlit candles,
she grins down into blue eyes.
Cheerfully asks
Who's this beautiful birthday girl?

Quivering hand searches for support
as she attempts the porch stairs.
Front door thrown open, she looks up
age leaves temporarily—
she hugs with surprising firmness.
Blue eyes, flowing blonde hair,
 cap, and gown.
Grandma reaches up, pats her cheek.
Glowing smile inquires
Who's this beautiful young woman?

She fixes her blonde hair quickly
in reflection on the institution door.
Walking down the corridor,
sterile air is thick with dead spirit.
Soft knock on doorframe announces arrival.
Blue eyes fall on the frail woman.
Sunken, lifeless eyes look up
from the wheelchair, and innocence shatters.
Blank stare asks,
Who are you?

Experienced

by Liz Lofgren

Midnight. Streetlamps dull
dilated eyes peer from shadows
He slinks from the alley haven
flicks away a menthol cherry

His head snaps at approaching noise
Body tense, the wanderer stares transfixed
at inexperienced strangers to the night

He is spotted, ears perk—voices hush
Encounter inevitable, they rush past him
clinging to cloaks of nescience in chilly air
Dismissed, he is left alone with thoughts
to wander his waking dream

Rescue
by Liz Lofgren

Flee vainly from nightmares—
shadows haunt my waking dream.

Held by bed-sheet noose,
swim in sweat—
jolt from drowning,
can't shake callous thoughts.

The brush of your hand
grabs mine in rescue,
your smile celestial,
exile morbid demons.

A whisper,
I love you.

Kiss my scarring tears,
caress your cheek.
I hold on to your smile
to stay afloat in the sea of your eyes.

Brief Eternity

by Liz Lofgren

Cruising backroads passing philosophy in a bowl,
midnight's glow from the dash
hangs lazily in haze.
Smiling eyes talk of no tomorrow—
temporary, nonetheless.

High beams grip the gravel road.
Hands embrace across the center consol,
so desperate for these seconds,
unwilling to let time seep through a sieve.

Eyes reflect subtle worry of numbered nights,
yet *every single night*
to fall in love *all over again*?

Then time is meaningless.

A crossroads appears through the dusty windshield—
quiet tears pray for coalesced destiny,

but chance of choosing a shared path
is a bigger miracle
than reaching up and touching stars.

Still-born
by Liz Lofgren

Final threads of being
cling to *her*.
Sobbing mother,
silent father
plead for yesterday
when little almond eyes
opened
only once
as if to say,
Just passing through.

Break-up
by Liz Lofgren

That feeling is back.
That one, like a bad cold,
like a stupor, disconnected
from the rest of the world.
A thousand parasites
devouring the senses
and the few things that could generate a smile.
The one that leaves mascara stains on the pillow,
lacerations from strangers' pity
at the sight of puffy, red eyes.
The one that makes you cry, and cry,
until dry heaves are met with a convulsive welcome.
The one that makes you question
the illegitimacy of self-mutilation
as a deliverance from abuse.
That one, hidden behind a curtain of bangs,
a way to meet the only aspiration—
to be unnoticeable, unrecognizable, incommunicable.
The one that sticks, of brooding panic
that no sense can be made, no escape
from endless undying emptiness.
That feeling is back.

The Old Man

by Liz Lofgren

Trash, junk, knick knacks, stuff, shit
The now-grown man sifted through piles, and boxes,
and piles of boxes,
sorting the memories of a life now gone.
Air Force pilot, rank 0-3 lieutenant.
He gazed at the Distinguished Flying Cross
and thumbed off the dust.
He held back a salty tear, and chuckled,
and softly said, "Oh dad . . . oh dad. . . ."

Decades later shit is finally being sorted,
and his son is put to the task
of deciding which memories are worth saving.
The once beautiful, great white farmhouse is now
a peeling, run-down ghost of this man's past.
The son pushed through molding furniture,
antique, unopened containers of food,
every *National Geographic* in print since the 50s,
and mountains of broken, useless family heirlooms.
He sees how his father lived out the rest of his life,
fought back a salty tear,
and softly said, "Oh dad . . . oh dad. . . ."

His father was a hard man.
He used whiskey to drown the horrors of the war.
His son was witness to many explosive tantrums,
a flip of the chair, a reach for the belt.
Shouts raged up through cracks in the floorboards.
He used to stare wide-eyed at the rigid war hero.
Yet, with a swell in his heart,
he recalled the day his father checked into rehab.

Back at a withered farm in the Kansas grasslands,
the son found the key to the closet in the study,
and opened it,
to be greeted with empty rum and beer bottles
piled to the knees. He picked one up.
40 years the old man had been lying.
The bottle slipped from limp hands,
and shattered along with his heart.
He choked back salty tears,
and chuckled,
and softly said, "Oh dad . . . oh dad. . . ."

Alvaro Archundia Perez

" Mijo, Por naturaleza Mexicanos son guerreros."

"Son, by nature Mexicans are warriors."

- My father, Alvaro Archundia Nava

#69

by Archundia Perez

It was **10:59**

I said hi
You said boyfriend
I said fuck him
You said go fall off a cliff

But it was you who fell
Onto my bed
Clothes generously donated to my floor
A cock so exotic
Is what you said
Your clit erected like my dick

That was the first time
First time you heard *Papi speaka Espanish*
Te encata cuando hablo en mi Español
You hung on to my enticing words
Words you didn't understand
More, more Is what you moaned

My room filled with music
Music of **47** missed calls and **22** messages
Your boyfriend thinking of you
You thinking of yourself
Your toes tingled
Your legs kept shaking
You couldn't stop
PAPI!
14 minutes
Felt like **55**

Any plans for tomorrow
Is what you said

You're just a Tuesday night
Now get the fuck out
Is what I said

It was just **12:57**

A Fatal Storm

by Archundia Perez

Terrifying thunder
Awakes the paranoid man
Out of breath again
Hostile storm-drops
Assault the two-faced window
Mutilating his inner peace

He wakes his wife

-"I can't sleep"
-"It's just a storm"
-"It's not just a storm"
-"Sweetheart it's nothing
Go back to sleep"
-"You're probably right"

The storm quiets
He goes to sleep

Piercing lighting
Betrays the man
Out of breath again
He slowly bleeds out
As the storm goes back to sleep

"A Survivor Once Told"

by Archundia Perez

The secret to surviving
Is to stay away from parasites
Parasites will be the end of you
Physically weaker than their host
Mentally stronger by far
There are many types
Some hurtful
Others lethal
Excessively, they'll stuff your insides
Seductively, they'll eat your children
Exhausting you
Until you are no longer useful
You'll watch in agony
As they find another host
Then brutally take your life
So remember
The secret to surviving
Stay away from women

Dear Jefe

by Archundia Perez

Be a man
Men are strong
Men don't cry

I was seven and fell of my bike
Scrapped my knee and came to you for comfort
Only thing out of your mouth
Did I give you permission to get hurt
Followed by the worst beating of 1994

Be a man
Men are strong
Men don't cry

You loved me
That is truth
But l could have learned without pain
You were the hardest working man in the Midwest
With nothing to show

My shirt ripped at school and I was embarrassed
My friend gave me one of his
I came home and it slapped you in the face
The clothes I give you aren't good enough
Were the words that pierced through me
Voice so terrifying made my tear ducts full
Only thing I could do was cry

Be a man
Men are strong
Men don't cry

You were a proud man and gave me all you could
Endless sacrifices fed my stomach and covered my back

Making me a man was your main concern
Weakness had no place in your bloodline

Be a man
Men are strong
Men don't cry

Now, time has claimed our years
Gray and with a cane you walk this land
A wise man
 veteran of life

I too have grown
Everything you inflicted on me
Reigns over my decisions

I am a man
I am strong
And I can't cry

Aren't you proud of me *Jefe*?
A tear will never claim this face
Until the day you die

Dear Senator
by Archundia Perez

Week 1 Month 1

Dear Senator,

My name is *Elias Avila*. I am 12 years old and a student at Madison middle school in Madison, NE. The reason I am writing you is because it's been a few days and I haven't seen my mother. She is an undocumented immigrant but her family are U.S. Citizens, my father, my two sisters, and myself. Why does my mother have to be in Mexico? I am writing you because you are a man in power. I'm also writing to the other senator, the representatives, and Mr. Bill Clinton. Please reply, I'll be waiting.

Sincerely,
a Nebraska

Child

Week 2 Month 3

Dear Senator,

This is *Elias Avila* again. I've been writing to you once every week and yet no response. My mother is still in Mexico and we don't know when she will be able to come back. I don't think you understand how much she is missed. We need her. I need her. We are falling apart. My father, bless his tired soul, is working everyday. Then he comes home to make us dinner. But he is lost without my mother. He is struggling to keep it together, but he still loses it. My sisters are suffering too. My older sister and my dad always argue. She is always gone and I have to hear about it from my dad. When she leaves, he takes it out on my. And when my diad is gone, she takes it out on me too. I need help and I'm asking you for something, please. I don't know what to tell my little sister anymore. She cries in my arms every night. She really misses my mother too. My dad has forces us to sleep together. He thinks somehow that will help keep the family together. My little sister sleeps in his bed and my dad and I on the floor. I hate sleeping on the floor. Please reply. Isn't our motto "Equality Before the Law" and this is a Nebraska child in need.

Sincerely,

a Nebraska

Child

Week 1 Month 6

Why the fuck can't you answer me? Huh?! I see that I am not your concern. Better yet, people who look like me are not your concern. Fuck you and fuck you people. The only thing you care about are sunscreen wearing motherfuckers like you. Don't worry gringo you don't have to respond to this one. I don't need help, especially from people like you. I know the truth now. I should thank you for opening my eyes. We are not equal. I'm not stupid anymore. "Equality Before the Law" what kind of bullshit is that? The world is fucked up, Nebraska is no different. I may live here. But I will never call it home. This place is for you and you can have it. But remember this you conservative racist motherfucker. One day I will grow up and be someone. Someone people like you should fear. You can take all our laws and put up your ass you *pinche culero*.

Without Equivocation,

the

FUCK nebraska Child

Deceived

by Archundia Perez

I loved you
I feel like a fool
We have a daughter
How could you be so cruel
Why did you fuck my sister
I trusted both of you
I can't believe my wife's a dike
I'm so disgusted by you

Erotic Sin
by Archundia Perez

Her sight taken from his shirt
A sweat flows from his forehead
She says no
No means yes
That is how she wants it

So humid he can't breath
Veins gorging like his cock
Undergarments stolen from her body
Skin fragments underneath desperate nails
She is a freak

Music so loud
She screams
He shouts
She cries
He slaps
She likes it rough

He touches
She flinches
She is a ticklish one

He impales her with conviction
His body screams pleasure
Hers cries RAPE!

Mexican American

by Archundia Perez

From East L.A.
America's Mexico
From Northeast Nebraska
White America
Mexican yet American
American yet Mexican

What am I?

Not Mexican
I have an American accent
Not American
I have a Mexican Accent
Raised Mexican
Lived American
Bruised for *mi* American
Fractured for my Mexican

I've tried to be accepted

Mexicans don't understand my problems
Americans can't comprehend my worries
Too Mexican for Americans
Too American for Mexicans

But now I know

My non-American heart pumps hot blood
Piss me off
I'll beat the American out of you
Uncle Sam would be proud
My non-Mexican eyes see bullshit
Piss me off
I'll be the Mexican out of you

Pancho Villa would be proud

 forever, a tattoo on my name

Mexican American

Mi Mariposa
by Archundia Perez

I try
But I can't
I constantly think of you
At times I feel like I succeeded
But a song, a phrase, or even a butterfly
Brings you back as if I failed
Seems like at anytime
I hear or see your name
I will never be sincerely happy
Until I'm with you
But that will never be
*Siempre estas en mi sue*ños
So I pray for no sleep
But I won't lie
when dream is my reality
I wish to never wake
Porque para siempre
Este Corazon will be yours

My World

by Archundia Perez

I want to give you a taste
Of a world I know
A world built of secrets

Where if I talked
Hundreds could be arrested by the end of the day

Where a man has dual identities
The call him Joe Suarez
We know him as *Jose Cabrera*

Where a man's age is a lie
He's 15
But his papers say 18
So he can work

Where the big yellow house on main
Can give you a new identity
Take $2000 and knock 7 times

Where half the marriages are nothing more
Than agreements and payoffs

Where I could get $10,000
To say she's my wife for 3 years

Where your mouth gets welded shut
 around the badge
For they are the enemy

Where you exchange words
Only to your own kind
For they understand your pain

Where names of *Coyotes*
Are treasured
Like a get out of jail card

Where you send your birth certificate
To your undocumented cousin
So he can pass through

Where if you say
La Migra
Thousands will drop their lives
And leave to create a new one

Where no matter how much
You hate a person
You never turn them in
For that is how your family lived

Where you get asked
For your documents
Just because of the way you look
For we are all wetbacks

Where houses get raided
And families torn apart
For we are a plague

Where they don't have enough handcuffs
So they dehumanize us
With zip ties

Where the instinct of survival
Is always a must
For we are always the hunted

Where the animosity of the white man
Is felt

Because we don't fit
Into their perfect white world

And where we have more secrets
Than we actually share
For it could
The safety and progress
Of *mi raza*
my race

Because this world is so deep
You must be born into it
In order to know
But you will never know
Cause we will never tell

THIS IS MY WORLD

Niño

by Archundia Perez

Finally ***Niño***, this is your time. Your time to cry. Cry to your heart's content. Butterflies in your stomach, emotional dispositions blooming from your domain. A smile lighting up from the shadows. Eyes filled with joyful tears. A blink, all you need is a blink ***Niño***. A blink for that long awaiting tear. The tear so desperately needed so many times. At last the tear that will vanish your fears with its salty stream. *Al fin….*the blink that was so desperately needed, dry, famished by the months of lost hope. Then you realized something ***Niño***. The butterflies in your stomach, an ache from the disgust of the failed system. The emotional dispositions blooming from your domain was not happiness or joy, but pain and anger erupting from your chaos. And the smile, an animal's reaction of displaying fangs right before the beast enters battle. ***Niño***, separated from your innocence and faith, you are no longer a *niño* but a man. An individual built from pain and struggles. Crying is not meant for you. You are to be strong when everyone else is fragile. Always be "*Macho*." But now it's time for your family and you to go home.

As the family leaves, the new man looks to his left as he sees the past. A scene too familiar for those walls. One more family torn apart by the same system that dismantled his. A father about to be sent away for committing a crime, the crime of being born on the wrong side of a river. A mother and daughter suffocated by their tears. And a boy, barely seeing age 10. His head too heavy, his body screaming "CRY." Yet no tears because that is how he was raised. Raised to show no weakness. His life drastically changing. Left with overwhelming responsibilities. A sister who cries yet believes daddy will come home tomorrow. The boy looks around, their eyes meet. The new man can see the boy's fear, his eyes struggling for help. But the new man can only look at him, his face emotionless, wanting to say something, something to help. But the new man just walked by with only one thought in his mind…"Good luck ***Niño***."

QUERIDO ADVERSITY

by Archundia Perez

MY BROTHER
MY RIVAL
MY MAIN *CARNAL*
ALWAYS YOU ARRIVE UNEXPECTEDLY
NEVER AT THE RIGHT TIME
WHEN I'M UP
YOU BRING ME DOWN
WHEN I'M DOWN
YOU DEPRESS ME TO DARKER REALMS
YOU HAVE MANY NAMES
TROUBLE, MISERY
ARE JUST A FEW YOU CLAIM
YOU HAVE CONQUERED MANY
TIME AFTER TIME
YOU'VE TRIED YOUR TRICKS ON ME
BUT HERE I AM
BLEEDING, IN PAIN
READY FOR OUR NEXT ENCOUNTER
WITH OPEN ARMS YOU WILL BE EMBRACED
FOR I AM A FIGHTER
YOU ARE MY ANGEL OF TORTURE
I AM YOUR ANGEL OF DEFEAT
YOUWILL ALWAYS RETURN
BUT REMEMBER THIS
WHEN IT COMES TO YOU AND ME
IN THE FIELD OF BATTLE,
SECOND BEST YOU'LL ALWAYS BE

No Gringo
by Archundia Perez

"It's ok"
"You can tell me what's wrong"
I can only look at him
Who is this white man
Why does he want to know
I didn't say anything
But I know I should
My dad is looking at me
I have to speak
Or else he will deal with me
The man turns to my sister
She is 10 and confused
He says,
"It's been 6 months"
"It's okay you can trust me"
No *gringo*
We were raised to never trust people who look like you
She begins to cry
Why did he make my sister cry
I turn to my father for reason
I'm confused
I am seeing a face
A face I've never seen
His lips are trembling
His nose flaring
Then I see his eyes
Guarded by a shield of tears
Who the fuck is this guy
Why is my family breaking
Immediately I notice
I too am breaking down
My eyes are flooded
I don't know what I'm feeling
Am I angry, sad?

confused
The room is cold
But I feel hot
WHO THE FUCK IS THIS MOTHERFUCKER
AND WHY DO I WANT TO CRY
OF COURSE I MISS MY MAMA
BUT YOU THE FUCK ARE YOU TO PRY
MY SISTER IN TORMENTING TEARS
MY FATHER IN SURPRISING FEARS
MY OLDER SISTER, TRAPPED IN THE STREET
COPING WITH ALCOHOL AND WEED
NOW YOU REALLY PISSED ME OFF YOU MOTHER-
FUCKER
I SHOULD JUST KIDNAP YOUR FUCKING MOTHER
SO INSTEAD OF WONDERING HOW I FEEL
YOU TOO CAN SUFFOCATE IN MY CONSTANT FEAR
NOW LOOK WHAT YOU'VE DONE
YOU FUCKING *GRINGO*
I FEEL LIKE A MONSTER
NOW I WANT TO KILL YOU
HIJO DE SU PUTA MADRE
I'M ONLY 12 YEARS OLD
BUT YOU WILL BE THE FIRST OLD MAN
TO ABSORB MY MEXICAN BLOWS
THAT'S RIGHT LOOK AT ME YOU FUCKING PUTO
SAY ONE WORD SO I CAN JUST EXPLODE ON YOU

Then the man said
"And how do you feel"
I want to say
My frustration has reached its LIMIT
I WANT TO CRY TO STRUGGLE THROUGH IT
But I am a man and men don't cry
So I take the biggest gulp of my fucking life
And with the calmest yet piercing tone
The boy said to the psychiatrist
"fuck you" and walked out the door.

Perfect life
by Archundia Perez

In the morning
He walked into work smiling
Greeted by all as he strolled to his office
Sir, to every person in the building

During lunch
He played golf with the Mayor
After, he fucked the Mayor's wife
Then for fun, smacked the bitch's titties
Why not, best ass and pussy in the city
Online, he checked his account
Still the richest man in town
"The luckiest man alive," they said
Desperately wanting to be him

When evening came
"It's late" he said
With a forced smile he shouted
"Have a wonderful evening
and I'll see you guys tomorrow."
He went home
And blew out his brains with the revolver

Thanksgiving Miracle

by Archundia Perez

1986
10 and homeless
Hungry and alone
Parents claimed by the epidemic
Coldest Thursday yet
November will soon be over
Then the snow will come
The streets are busy
Society walks by
Thinking "poor little boy"
But they keep walking
A man approaches
You hungry?
Come with me
Everything will be alright
The boy looks at the man
His smile
Too persuasive
Too comforting for these times
The boy followed
First bath in months
Fresh clean clothes
The boy sits at the table
Most food he's ever seen
The boy eats
Feasting
Enough to keep full for days
It was the boy's best day
Couldn't ask for any better
***

Suddenly
A stroking motion against his back
The man says
Do you want to see something?

The boy doesn't know what to do
It's normal what you're feeling
Just relax
The boy finds it difficult to relax
Here, you must be uncomfortable
Let's take yours off
The boy doesn't want to
The man says
Follow me
They go into a room
And the man locks the door
NOW BEND OVER BOY
The boy begins to beg
please don't, I don't want to
WHAT, YOU THOUGHT THIS WAS FREE
He grabs the boy
The boy tries to resist
But the man is too strong
He strikes the boy with his left
The boy's sight turns red
Then the man splits the boy with his erected blade
Thrusting fiercely
Ambushing the boy
Like hyenas on a helpless prey
Wild and unforgiving
The boy screams
Sending chills through the walls
The scent of blood
Delivering disturbing signals to the man
Urging him to impale with tormenting force
Veins filled with rage
Slaying with no remorse
The boy finally stops crying
The man finishes with one last evil piercing
He pulls out his weapon
Drenched in the boy's soiled innocence
Get up boy

…nothing
I SAID GET UP BOY
…again no movement from the boy
His fragile state couldn't endure any longer
His body laid on the bed
Lifeless
He drags the deadweight body
Buries in his garden
Pats the final dirt with his shovel
And whispers,
Happy Thanksgiving

Natural Selection

by Archundia Perez

Homeless life
Every man for himself

A dollar twenty-one
His life's savings
To buy a bottle
For a temporary cure
Hands in his pockets
One keeping warm
The other gripping a rusty blade

Homeless life
Every man for himself

Society passes by
Faces guided by malicious eyes
Around the corner
A little homeless girl
Terrified, abandoned
A sparkling necklace around her neck
Easy prey

Homeless life
Every man for himself

He approaches the girl
Looks her in the eyes
This is too easy
Grabs her necklace
Tucks it in her shirt
People will kill you for that
I'm hungry she says
He looks at her
His face un-responsive

Takes out his hand
Gives her a dollar twenty-one
Go buy yourself a hotdog

Homeless life
Every man for himself

A guardian angel
Walks away
Thirsty and hungry
That evening
He slits a stranger's throat
And takes his Nikes

Homeless life
Every man for himself

Transition

by Archundia Perez

Paycheck

Cash it

Spend it

New hat
New dickies
New whites
Fat laces with the metal tips

California
Kriss kross
Old school
Loop *y* loop
Shit,
Bowtie

19

On top of the world

Tonight

Game night

Game tools

Bubblicious
Toothpicks
Cool water
Variety pack
Fuck climax control
I need sensation

Beer pong
Keg stands
Sloppy sluts
Puff puff pass
Crazy night
Go to sleep

Good dreams

***

Paycheck

Cash it

Spend it

Oatmeal
Onezees
Huggies
Off brand milk with the red cap

Nasty smell
Dirty diaper
Diaper rash
Soothing cream
Shit,
Johnson's

22

Trying to keep up with the world

Tonight

Game night

Game tools

Peek-a-boo
Batman blankey
Lula byes
Read books
Fuck wheels on the bus
I need sleep

Goodnight *mijo*
Jefe loves you
Kid tucked in
Goodnight kiss
Crazy night
Got to sleep

Dream great.

James Thompson

"It is better to write for the self and have no public,
than to write for the public and have no self."

- Cyril Connolly

A Man's Perspective

by James Thompson

What's a bitch? A female dog.
Us men wish they were that loyal.
These chicks are quick to flip,
the nasty ones you call flippa dips.

Most will eat a man's heart,
something like a cannibal.
That's why their called bitches,
cuz they act like animals.

I met a lady who said she doesn't trust men.
I thought I had the antidote.
Maybe instead being an asshole,
I'll be sweet like cantaloupe.

In my mouth she left a
sour taste but for some strange
reason, I still smile
every time I see her face.

Over the years I've learned
neva chase a dog, they'll just run faster.
Beware some girls will give you
viruses, just like napster.

So fellas, If you're a good man
and love is what you're after.
I say good luck, get on your knees,
and pray like a pastor.

A Thin Line

by James Thompson

A couple months after the split,
I found out you were due in nine.
It seems you started a new life.
I have no clue what to do with mine.

I know we had to split
Because you lost my trust.
You cheated on me
and my ego you crushed.

I still have love for you
but I don't know why.
Sometimes I wish we never met
or that you'd just die.

I was once filled with love
now I am full with hate.
You're pregnant by another man
and I can't even date.

From under this love spell
I want to escape.
Today, I truly realized there is
a thin line between love and hate.

B

by James Thompson

I'm close to my fam
Especially my kid sis
No disrespect when I say the B word
But she's a real bitch
We used to beef hard
Steady ballin our fist
Now instead of pushing and punchin
On the cheek it's a kiss
When we lived under the same roof
We barely even spoke
Now we talk on the phone
Just to laugh and joke
I didn't know it
But back then
I was her role model
So she started passing blunts
And throwin down bottles
Even afta she knows I've done wrong
She looks up to me still
For her I will do anything
Including the word kill

Boys in Blue

by James Thompson

Police put on badges and say
they're here to make a difference.
But they walk around in blue
and carry guns too. So tell me
what's the difference?

Between thugs and them,
because they are the same to me.
Both of them are something I
will could never be.

They both ride through the hood late
at night. Goons bumping music
and pig's lights are shinning bright.
They both rob and shoot! Keep
ya head on a swivel or they might
end up robbing you. And they both
stay with heat, the boys' keep it on their hips
and street soldiers' pistols are under their seats.

Even when shits bad they thrive
in they our community.
Both try to stay low
so they hide in our community.
They keep the block so hot,
snow melts when it lands.
All I see is red and blue
lights, body bags, and cuffs on black hands.

Living Colored

by James Thompson

Some of us can only see green
We stay strapped with black gats
Equipped with red beams

Why?

Because we rob or serve white
Don't get caught
Because you might just serve life

That will leave our mothers so blue
But it is better than being left red
Because that means death-- has chose you

Man Made
by James Thompson

Dark brown eyes give off a darker glare
Blind to your forced smiles
Ears deaf to your awkward greetings
Smile more crooked than my hat
Chest swelled up like fresh breast implants
Hands balled up like a bad poem
Fist leave eyes Lakers' colors
Thoughts darker than my skin
Clique more savage than hungry hyenas
Brain dead like half my homies
Spirit gone like my father
Derogatory words pierce my victims like hollow tips
Heart so cold you'd get frost bite if you touched it
Can't help it--
Man made me this way

Man of the House

by James Thompson

If a nigga must gangbang
to slang cain
just to stack change
Is his life worth anything?

A Judge
Willing to dictate
His fate
20 to life is his rate

He sits behind bars
Cuz he sold dope
And stole cars
His heart so scared
So his demeanor
Rock hard

A teen forced to
Raise two kids
Now he is off
Doing two bids
Must serve more years
Than he's lived

Not close to perfect
But far from worthless
To put clothes
On his bros
He'd go shirtless

Now to see them He must set a date
He's no longer the man of the house
His brothers belong to the state

Monday

by James Thompson

She hears a loud cart coming
from around the corner.
A freshly shaved man appears
from behind the rusty milk bossy.
Dressed in a faded blue shirt
dirty khakis,
and air max's
that have seen a few front line battles.

He brings his bossy to a halt
a few feet short
of her bright yellow cart.
Immediately he is greeted
with a smile.
Her hair in a messy bun
sporting a dingy yellow workout shirt
and old grey sweats turned inside out
which he notices she fills out well.

They say excuse me
simultaneously and attempt
to move out of the way.
Only to both step in
the same direction.
After side stepping a few times
he finally navigates his way around her.

She looks back with her most seductive smile
and walks out of his life for the first time.

Sea of Life

by James Thompson

As I doggy paddle through life
it's struggle to stay afloat.
People point and laugh
as the pass by on a boat.

I'm repeatedly hit
with wave after wave.
I'm tired of funerals
visiting grave after grave.

I'm exhausted
my body begs me to stop.
But if I listen
to the bottom I'll drop.

After a prayer for strength
some hope is found.
I got keep swimming
because only the weak will drown.

What's Her Name

by James Thompson

When I look at her
I'm enamored

By her bright whites
With her I feel safe
Like a child with a night light

I was told

Never trust

A women again

But my feelings
Make me

Wanna be

More than a friend
All day I fiend

For her company
I'm diggin' her --
Is she lovin' me?

Adrian White

"Our greatest glory is not in never falling,
but in getting up everytime we do."

- Confucius

Her Beauty

by Adrian White

drives me insane
trying to blemish
her perfection
in my brain
has proved inane

her love I must obtain
for it's worth more
than any fame.

How
not the slightest notion
but I keep trying
immense devotion.

Critical choice to make
let love innovate?
Slightly hesitate
her heart's fate
I deliberate.

Physical attraction
devastating
captivating

beyond satisfaction
I'm clearly impassioned
an effectual fashion.

Hate
by Adrian White

Hate infused with
immense corruption
calm spawn
of absolute destruction.

Malice incased
in solitary confinement
rationality?
Can't seem to find it
eyes once wide
slightly blinded
rage implodes
from negativity under-minded.

Soul sold to defiance
logic lost
on an island
control the beast
that lies immanent
his new assignment.

Hood But Not Hood

by Adrian White

I from the hood
where real is *real*
niggas that squeal
impaled with steel

yes the hood
but here's the deal
that very *real*
that makes hood
hood
didn't appeal

Jack-boys
concealed by night
bout to leave a nigga *left*
so they can get *right*
grind
until money reach
excessive height
no time for fear
or fright
scary?
Hell, this is life.

I Promise

by Adrian White

Thought process
extra cautious
clearly flawless
divine goddess

beautiful yet modest
I'm positively
the man you always wanted
heart broken
past haunted.

Treated nothing less
than a queen
honest.

Anything to make her happy
I promise.

I Will Make You Feel

by Adrian White

I will make you feel
like you've never imagined
continuous sensuous pleasures
you couldn't possibly fathom

Immanent passions hatching
from our bodies latching
desires erupting
you'd think the titans were clashing
yearning for each other
matching.

My lips whisk down your neck
so brisk
your compelled to bit your lip.

I kiss the spot
slightly under your hip
penetrate slowly
your eyes insist

so I enter extensively into your abyss

eyes closed
biting your fist
orgasms rapidly consist
so blissful
your forced to reminisce

Relieved
by Adrian White

these emotions
were not chosen
thawed heart
 was once frozen

her presents soothes
I am the being
which her smile moves
heartbreak removed
indecision too.

eyes possessing the power
to heal wounds
with haste
sooner then soon

shield my fate
from confining doom
resuscitate hope
annihilate gloom

iv'e been reprieved
of my reason to grieve
although ive been bereaved

god has blessed me as if I just sneezed.

Running Through My Mind

by Adrian White

running through my mind
ive loss track of time
soon her body
will lye next to mine

when we kiss
compelling chills up my spine
my soul shakes
like magic
of some kind

shes relentlessly supportive
withdrawing her from my thoughts
has proved abortive

She's Walking by Magic
by Adrian White

Attempt to speak
thoughts flee
she passes me
my eyes study her naturally
lust leaking lavishly
emotions ravaging savagely
irrational passion peaks
yet I remain discreet

brilliance glows incandescently

Special Girl
by Adrian White

heart annihilated
deceptive world
cherished beauty
sacred pearl

her heartbreak
I can
rehabilitate
to seal away
her tarnished fate
I wouldn't hesitate
the mending of her heart
I wish to participate
deliver love that devastates
take action sooner than late
alleviate her
from this anguished state

The Pain
by Adrian White

The pain
seems to exist rapidly
a blunt impact
from a blind tragedy.

If my enemies saw me
in this feeble state
the apparent anguish
would sustain them
they'd laugh
at how the pain
contains him
cheer
at how the unease
detains him
praise
the way the agony shames him

9:00 am
staring at a bottle of Southern Comfort
hoping to ease his discomfort

pleading
for solace
while marinating
in a state of soul crush.

Distress seems to find him
withered and lonely
misery confines him

The Source

by Adrian White

I really need you to see
that this is in fact critical to me
by any means I'll do anything
to make you believe
even if it means a second-time bereaved
I need you to comprehend
what I mean

it's like your smile radiates a contagious gleam

Now we're both smiling
butterflies inside are piling.

You compel a deep seated passion
that even the most creative mind couldn't imagine,
persistently feeling emotions I'd never fathom
existed consistently
but my words affect insufficiently
so desperately
I search for my deficiency,
and instantly
find the source of inconsistency.

David Dietz

"If you think you're free, there's no escape possible."

—Ram Dass

Me
by David Dietz

I'm no stranger to pain or the game I thrive in the rain
sometimes I wish I could explain
the thoughts in my brain
I feel insane and deranged when lookin' at lames
but there's more of them than me they the norm guess that I'm strange
if that's the case well fuck it then so be it
its cold in the war you can call me a Soviet
I smoke for my stress I don't dub I OZ it
and I face all my beef straight up I don't flee it
heart hard and cold like water below freezin'
stay like that never changin' for no reason
regardless of situation never for no breezy
only bitch I love is fillin' up my bleezy
flow got you feelin' me now come on don't it
title best rapper you know I own it
war with me on the mic aids you don't want it
and I only smoke the best weed homie my guy grow it
if the buds ain't purple or red I don't blow it
if I ain't got henny or crown I don't po it
fear like a shy bitch's titties I don't show it
bein' pussy is a foreign concept I don't know it
this is grown folks affairs you children just shouldn't meddle
general in the streets decorated with medals
detrimental to mental health when holdin' the metal
a rebel who revels in questionable endeavors
leave 'em bleedin' needin'
special medical chemicals
terrible technical technique
punchlines incredible
ya see I'm a nightmare
I don't ever fight fair
hit you leave you right there
I won't even might care
colder than a white bear

rippin' not a slight tear
my lines hard as frozen steel you a ripe pear
I'm ill and a villain who chillin' with people dealin'
whips that I'm wheelin' leave bitches kneelin' and willing
I'm feelin like the feeling that they catch come from the fillins
I drill 'em
you can see that I'm real and my skill when I'm killing.

Better
by David Dietz

my future lookin bright you could say that its flashin'
I been blessed by the man that they thrashed in the Passion
daily routine starts with puffin and passin'
fuck it that's all day
living room look like Pompeii
we smokin' bomb hay look at the ashes
dash to the lab lay a track and I smash it
all for the love of grabbin' asses and cash and
I love to see the smiles on the faces of the masses
sticky in my blunt crown in my glasses
bitches all want me like some backstage passes
haters can't see me they got Ray Charles glasses
I'm just trying to knock this rhyme out like Cassius
greatest of all time
I'm with a small dime
she know she all mine
she can take it all night
but I don't love her though
dick is a lethal weapon you can call it Danny Glover ho
always wear a rubber though
put that on my mother yo
I don't wanna end up on a stretcher under covers yo
now where was I the weed got me spaced out
never met George but I can't feel my face now
got me high got me stuck like paste wow
I feel like I'm in outer space now
now am I talkin' bout the weed and how high I am
or am I talkin' bout the flow and how fly I am
trick question both are correct
all I ever wanted to get in this life was respect
so when I grab a pen I'm comin' straight for the neck
its carnage watchin' me spit is like watching a wreck
I mean its nasty but you just can't look away
I lost a piece of my mind when my homie was took away
I wish that he could hear me I ain't never like to spit like this

this page a virgin it ain't never been ripped like this
everybody else's rhymes is foreplay I'm straight fuckin'
everybody say that they got bitches but they straight cuffin'
sayin' you the shit but when backed up you don't dump nothin'
frontin' that you down for robbin' hoods but u just friar tuckin'
the difference is I am the shit and your just shitty
my words are a masterpiece yours ain't even pretty
fuck with me the gun go bang bang I call it chitty
I show you rage anger and malice but never pity
I'm a whole fuckin' continent your just a city
you're about as hard as liquid soap and I'm so acidic

Curveball
by David Dietz

he fucked this bitch often it was easy after a couple shots
soon as his dick softened started havin' second thoughts
but then the phone rang "sup fag"
"ha don't even play yo"
"what it do"
"where you at pussy I need that yayo"
slap the bitches ass "grab ya shit it's time to step ho"
watchin' as she throw on her dress and her stilettos
"my bad homie give me 10 and I'll be at the spot"
"well hurry the fuck up man I'm tryin' to get this guap"
he threw on some pants grabbed the duffle hopped in the drop
heater underneath his tee cuz there haters on the block

little did he know that his transaction had been compromised
the bitch that he was creeping with was undercover in disguise
casing him for months stacking evidence for his demise
he thought he was comin' up but was in for a surprise

he knocked three times rang the bell once
the door swung open and he could smell blunts
greeted with a handshake native to his clique
"me and Money Mike are in the back, you got the bricks?"
"nah I forgot 'em muhfucka shit what you think"
"watch ya little smart ass mouth"
"man what you got to drink"

surveillance now confirming that the suspect has arrived
with a duffle bag in tow the operation is live
"agent Bryant agent Meyers your going in as the buyers
the goal is apprehend these suspects
and try to find their suppliers"
"grab the money make sure your guns off safety"
"complete the transaction and we'll bring you home safely"

he heard knocks at the door but something wasn't quite right

125

then caught movement out the corner of his eye sight
yellow letters black jackets
yells out "fuckin' fed faggots!"
let off sixteen into the copper till they toppled backwards
Money Mike trippin' like" what the fuck is you on"
he yelled out" its a setup you got pigs all over yo lawn"
they all had 2 strikes it was the bottom of the ninth inning
so they all walked out the front door guns drawn
just grinning

Help
by David Dietz

I'm nasty when I spit
like a hiccupping baby
When I hiccup I taste crazy
covered in gravy
Hi, I'm Davie
a.k.a. the escapee
mental ward missin' its star patient
Save me
I'm a sick and twisted criminal
usin' digital digits to put a fidgetin' midget in a condition that's
critical
Ever since the umbilical
I've been rotten and cynical
You witnessin' a villain who
wishes he was killin' you
As I'm sitting here
remembering
memories of
dismembering
everything I could get my hands on
I'm such a clever thing
Never been indicted
just excited
by frightened eyes widenin'
grip tightenin'
live siphonin'
A man in my position
envisions many decisions
having visions
of revisions
being made to circumcisions
playing physician
incisions without precision
Repugnant thoughts
abundant

redundant in my
succumbin' to
undulating covers covered in someone's woman
Cut up
It's terrifying
how I'm eyeing her
lying in lye and frying
crying as I'm
tying the knot
climbing high and
diving
into the noose I use to loose a few shoots of juice
then I loosen it
Collapsing and laughing
while having
fantasies stabbing
somebody's
faculty grabbing
onto the
balcony and jumping

CPSIA information can be obtained at www.ICGtesting.com
Printed in the USA
LVOW062248181212

312281LV00001B/28/P